INTERMITTI

For B_

*A Complete Selection of Super Satisfying Recipes
for your Alternate-Day Fasting*

Pamela Palmer

no scenarios in which the publisher or the original author of this work can be in any fashion deemed liable for any hardship or damages that may befall them after undertaking information described herein.

Additionally, the information in the following pages is intended only for informational purposes and should thus be thought of as universal. As befitting its nature, it is presented without assurance regarding its prolonged validity or interim quality. Trademarks that are mentioned are done without written consent and can in no way be considered an endorsement from the trademark holder.

TABLE OF CONTENTS

Introduction

Intermittent Fasting is a form of nutrition that alternates between a fixed fasting period and a time of normal food intake. Daily food intake is restricted. This diet is based on the principle that the human body can be cleaned naturally. As a result, he recovers and is strengthened, whereby the body functions can be carried out optimally. Intermittent fasting can be implemented in different ways. The shortest form includes short fasts lasting less than 24 hours. Longer forms include fasting periods of several days. For the body to recover, it is not only important when you eat in intermittent fasting. For the best result for the body and mind, it is also important which foods are consumed.

This diet has become popular over the years. It's a meal plan that you move back and forth between feeding and fasting periods. You have the option to plan your fasting and non-fasting periods. During those non-fasting times, take water. It is not necessary to do intermittent fasting every other day to lose weight; you can do this at least twice a week.

On an intermittent fasting diet, you are allowed to eat whatever you need during times when you are not fasting. Of course, on the off chance that you're hoping to get back in shape, you should stick to healthy foods and stay away from those that will nullify the whole procedure. It is necessary to consume sugars during this period, as they help digest fat. When you fast, drinking water is deeply empowering, as staying hydrated encourages you to get back into shape faster. One can go a long time without nourishment, but not without water.

There are many different versions of intermittent fasts, and you need to choose the method that suits you the most. Intermittent fasting can help you lose weight, burn body fats, protect you against disease, and has various other benefits as well.

While it is true that intermittent fasting is comparatively more straightforward than other forms of dieting, it is still a significant change in one's lifestyle that may or may not be difficult for you. You may struggle in the beginning. Your body will soon get accustomed to fasting. Regardless, here are a few tips that will make the overall fasting experience simpler.

All you have to keep in mind is the number of calories you are consuming per meal. Meals that have low carbs content are ideal because they, in turn, have low caloric content as well. Having more lean meats, fruits, and vegetables is ideal together with grains too.

Learn as many recipes as possible and prepare them for yourself to better manage the ingredients being used. You can even do a meal prep whereby you take one day to prepare the meals you wish to eat during the coming week. One reason to go for fast food is that it is readily available. Preparing your meals in advance can help you cover this.

Intermittent Fasting Recipes

Avocado Egg Wrapped in Raw Ham

Time required:
15 minutes

Servings: 01

INGREDIENTS	STEPS FOR COOKING

1 small avocado (approx. 150 g)

1 egg

50 g raw ham

10 g coconut oil

1. Put the egg in a saucepan and fill it with warm water. Bring the water to a boil. Let the egg boil for 9 minutes, until it is hard.

2. Halve the avocado and remove the stone. Separate the pulp from the avocado peel with a tablespoon.

3. Peel the egg and place it in the avocado. Seal the avocado tightly and wrap the thinly sliced raw ham around it.

4. Heat coconut oil in the pan and fry the avocado all over. Serve the avocado with fresh salad.

Baked Apple Porridge

Time required:
25 minutes

Servings: 06

25 g tender wholegrain oat flakes

1 tbsp flaxseed

200 ml almond milk (or coconut water)

100 g low-fat cottage cheese or natural yogurt / kefir)

1 tbsp chopped nuts (e.g. walnuts or almonds)

50 g raisins

1 apple

50 ml apple juice

1 squirt of lemon juice

1. Put the oat flakes and linseed with the almond milk in a saucepan and simmer over a low heat for 2-3 minutes until both are swollen. Let cool down briefly.

2. Add the cottage cheese (alternatively use natural yoghurt or kefir), cinnamon, nuts and raisins and mix well.

3. Wash, peel, core and finely chop the apples. Simmer together with a splash of lemon juice and the apple juice in a small saucepan for about 10 minutes until the apple juice has evaporated.

4. Put the porridge with the baked apple in a bowl and enjoy warm.

Almond Smoothie

Time required:
5 minutes

Servings: 01

INGREDIENTS	STEPS FOR COOKING

1 cup Unsweetened coconut milk

1 Tablespoon Chia Seeds

1 Tablespoon Peanut or Almond Butter

3 pieces Ice

1. Add all the ingredients to your blender and puree until completely smooth. Add more coconut milk if you need a thinner smoothie.

2. Serve!

Croissant Bake with Cheese and Ham

Time required:
45 minutes

Servings: 08

INGREDIENTS	STEPS FOR COOKING

Butter, for the dish

3-4 tsp Dijon mustard

8 plain croissants, cut in half lengthways

8 slices of ham

250g Comté cheese, grated

4 eggs

300ml whole milk

1 cup of Paysan breton french sea salt cream cheese

150ml of double cream

1 tbsp of ground black pepper

1. Butter a wide 35cm skillet pan and/or ovenproof dish and heat the oven to 180°C.

2. Spread a thin layer of Dijon mustard on each half of the croissant and finish with a slice of ham. Distribute the grated Comté among the eight croissants and place them at the bottom of the serving dish.

3. Whisk together the eggs, whole milk, 34% cream cheese (save the remainder for later) and double cream in a big jug or bowl, seasoning well with ground black pepper that is fresh.

4. Pour over the croissants and set aside for 10 minutes to take up more of the liquid.

INGREDIENTS	STEPS FOR COOKING
A bunch of chopped chives	5. Preheat the oven and bake the croissants for 25-30 minutes, and till golden brown and bubbling. 6. Serve quickly after inserting the remaining cream cheese and minced chives.

Chia Pudding with Fruit

Time required:
2 hours

Servings: 02

INGREDIENTS

400g chia seeds

400g blueberries

2 vanilla pods

2 bananas

2 pinches of stevia

4 apples

4 kiwis

600ml almond milk

STEPS FOR COOKING

1. Cut the vanilla pods open, scrape out the pulp with a spoon and then with chia seeds, Stevia, almond milk in a bowl give and mix.

2. Put the mixture in the refrigerator for 2 hours, then stir the pudding and wash the fruit, cut it and then serve it together.

Coco Cinnamon-Packed Pancakes

Time required:
35 minutes

Servings: 02

INGREDIENTS

2 eggs

2½ tbsp. of organic coconut flour

¼ cup of milk substitute with hydrogenated vegetable oil (or almond milk)

1 tbsp. of baking soda

½ tbsp. of cinnamon

½ tbsp. of baobab powder

2 tbsp. of organic coconut flower syrup

STEPS FOR COOKING

1. In a salad bowl, mix the coconut flour, baobab powder, cinnamon, and baking soda.

2. Add the beaten eggs, the almond milk, and the coconut syrup. Then let the dough rest for 40 minutes.

3. Cook the pancakes in a hot pan with coconut oil.

4. Dress the pancakes with raspberries/blueberries or almonds.

Low-Carb Cheese & Bacon Stuffed Meat Pies

Time required: 55 minutes

Servings: 04

INGREDIENTS

500 g ground beef (1.1 lb.)

4 large slices bacon, chopped (120 g/ 4.2 oz.)

1 small brown onion, chopped (g/ oz.)

1 tbsp. coconut amines (15 ml)

2 tbsp. tomato sauce/passata (30 ml)

1 cup beef stock or broth (240 ml/ 8 Fl. oz.)

½ tsp xanthan gum

Pie crust

STEPS FOR COOKING

1. Cut the bacon into small strips and dice the onion. Add to a skillet, along with the ground beef. Cook until just browned. Add coconut aminos, pasta, beef stock, and xanthan gum and stir well to combine. Bring to boil then reduce the heat and simmer for 30 minutes. Remove from the heat and let cool. Once mixture is cool, heat oven to 200 °C/ 390 °F (fan assisted). Prepare the pie crust.

2. Place the cheeses and cream cheese into a large bowl and microwave for 1 minute. Remove and stir, then return for another 30 seconds. Repeat this once more. Add the almond meal, onion powder, and eggs and mix well until you have a soft dough. Divide

2 ¼ cups shredded mozzarella cheese (250g/8.8oz)

1 cup 2 tbsp. shredded Edam cheese (125g/4.4oz)

1/3 cup 1 tbsp. full-fat cream cheese (100g/3.5oz)

1½ cups Almond flour (150g/5.3 oz.)

2 large eggs

1 tsp. onion powder

6 small chunks of sharp cheddar

into four parts and sit one portion aside. Cut each of the remaining three portions in half and then flatten them out into large circles (you will have a total of six circles.)

3. Spray a six-hole oversized muffin pan and press the dough into each cup, making sure to leave overhang at the top as the dough will shrink while cooking.

4. Bake for 10 minutes. Remove and spoon some filling into each cup. Press a chunk of cheddar into the center.

5. Then top with the remaining filling. Divide the reserved dough into six pieces and flatten out into lids. Lay the lid on top of the pies and gently press around the edges to seal.

6. Cut a couple of steam vents in top of each pie. Return to the oven for 10-15 minutes until golden brown on top. Eat warm, with sugar-free ketchup if you want to feel very Australian.

Cinnamon and Pecan Porridge

Time required:
2 minutes

Servings: 02

INGREDIENTS

1 cup unsweetened coconut milk

¼ cup almond butter

1 tbsp coconut oil, melted

2 tbsp whole chia seeds

2 tbsp hemp seeds

¼ cup pecans, chopped

¼ cups walnuts, chopped

¼ cups unsweetened and toasted coconut

1 tsp cinnamon

STEPS FOR COOKING

1. Put all the ingredients to the Instant Pot and mix.

2. Cover and cook for 9 minutes on high pressure.

3. When done, release the pressure naturally and remove the lid. Serve and enjoy!

Asian Salad

Time required:
15 minutes

Servings: 04

INGREDIENTS	STEPS FOR COOKING

INGREDIENTS

1 pound ground beef

1 tablespoon sriracha

2 tablespoons coconut aminos

2 garlic cloves, peeled and minced

10 ounces coleslaw mix

2 tablespoon sesame seed oil

Salt and ground black pepper, to taste

1 teaspoon apple cider vinegar

1 teaspoon sesame seeds

STEPS FOR COOKING

1. Heat up a pan with the oil over medium heat, add the garlic, and brown for 1 minute.

2. Add the beef, stir, and cook for 10 minutes. Add the slaw mixture, toss to coat, and cook for 1minute.

3. Add the vinegar, sriracha, coconut aminos, salt, and pepper, stir, and cook for 4 minutes.

4. Add the green onions and sesame seeds, toss to coat, divide into bowls, and serve.

INGREDIENTS

STEPS FOR COOKING

*1 green onion,
chopped*

Soup with Tomatoes, Peppers and Parmesan Strips

Time required:
45 minutes

Servings: 01

INGREDIENTS

½ onion

1 bunch of basil

1/2 tbsp olive oil

100 g peeled tomatoes (canned)

150 ml vegetable stock

1 teaspoon dried rosemary

30 g parmesan cheese

1 tbsp crème fraiche

salt

pepper

STEPS FOR COOKING

1. Preheat the oven to 200 C. Line the baking sheet with parchment paper. Cut the parmesan into fine strips.

2. Place the parmesan on the baking sheet and put it in the oven. Bake it on medium heat for 4-5 minutes, until the parmesan has melted and the edges start to brown. Take the baking sheet out of the oven and let the parmesan cool down.

3. Set the oven to 250 C. Cut the peppers in half. Core and wash them. Place the halves skin side up on the baking sheet. Bake them on the top rail for 10 minutes, until the skin gradually turns black and blisters. Take out the baking

sheet. Cover it with a wet towel and let the peppers cool.

4. In the meantime, peel and chop the onion. Wash the basil. Dry it and pluck the leaves off. Heat the olive oil in a saucepan and fry the onion in it over medium heat for 2 minutes. Add the canned tomatoes and vegetable stock to the pot. Add the basil and rosemary and bring the whole thing to a boil. Let the broth boil for 10 minutes.

5. In the meantime, peel off the skin of the peppers. Add the pulp to the soup. Puree the soup and bring it to a boil. Season them with salt and pepper.

6. Arrange the soup in a deep plate. Add the crème fraiche and garnish with the baked parmesan.

Savoy Cabbage Potato Stew

Time required:
55 minutes

Servings: 04

INGREDIENTS

800 g savoy cabbage

800 g potatoes

4 carrots

2 onions

1 liter of broth

1 teaspoon caraway seeds

4 tbsp sunflower oil

4 tbsp various herbs

1 teaspoon nutmeg

1 teaspoon cayenne pepper Salt pepper

STEPS FOR COOKING

1. Sauté the onion in a saucepan with oil until translucent. Cut the savoy cabbage into fine strips and the carrots into thin slices. Peel and dice the potatoes.

2. Steam everything together for a few minutes. Pour in the broth, add the caraway seeds and bring the soup to the boil.

3. Cover and simmer for about 20 minutes and add the herbs you want. Season to taste with salt and pepper.

Papaya and Apple Salad

Time required:
15 minutes

Servings: 02

INGREDIENTS

1 orange

10g walnuts

1 papaya

1 pinch of cinnamon

1 apple

2 tablespoons lemon juice

STEPS FOR COOKING

1. peel papaya, remove seeds and in pieces cut apple core and cut into pieces.

2. Then roughly chop the walnuts.

3. All together in a bowl give and with lemon drizzle.

Chicken Roasted with Indian Spices

Time required:
1 hour 10
minutes

Servings: 02

INGREDIENTS

1 medium chicken

2 tbsp. of vegetable oil

1 tsp of ground turmeric

1 tsp of ground coriander

1 tsp of cumin seeds

2 sliced limes,

1 green or red chili, deseeded & sliced

1 big thinly sliced garlic clove,

Salt and freshly ground black pepper

Fresh coriander sprigs, to serve

STEPS FOR COOKING

1. Heat oven at 200°C.

2. Then insert chicken into roasting tin.

3. Mix the turmeric, oil, coriander, & cumin seeds in a mixing bowl.

4. Cover the bird with the foil & roast it for ninety minutes to 1hr 40 minutes. Remove the foil 20 minutes before the end of the cooking period and add lime wedges, chili, and garlic.

5. Insert a sharp knife through the thickest portion of the chicken to see if it's completely cooked. There must be no pink juices visible. Cook for a few minutes longer if possible.

6. Before slicing, cover the chicken with the foil and let it rest for 10 minutes. It can be served with turmeric

potatoes after garnishing with fresh coriander.

Lamb Chops in Mint Cream Sauce

Time required:
55 minutes

Servings: 04

INGREDIENTS	STEPS FOR COOKING

INGREDIENTS

4 lamb chops

2 tablespoons of extra-virgin olive oil

1 cup of homemade low-sodium beef broth

2 tablespoons of fresh dill, chopped

¼ cup of fresh mint, chopped

1 tablespoon of freshly squeezed lemon juice

2 tablespoons of heavy whipping cream

STEPS FOR COOKING

1. Season the lamb ribs with sea salt and freshly cracked black pepper.

2. Press the "Sauté" setting on your Instant Pot and add the olive oil. Once hot, add the lamb ribs and sear for 3 minutes or until brown.

3. Pour in the beef broth. When the cooking is done, naturally release the pressure for 10 minutes, then quick release the remaining pressure. Carefully remove the lid.

4. In a blender, add the fresh dill, mint, lemon juice, heavy whipping cream. Blend until smooth.

5. Transfer the lamb chops to serving plates and top with the mint cream sauce.

INGREDIENTS	STEPS FOR COOKING
Fine sea salt and freshly cracked black pepper (to taste)	

Pulled Pepper-Lemon Loins

Time required:
25 minutes

Servings: 04

INGREDIENTS	STEPS FOR COOKING

INGREDIENTS

½ stick of butter

1 large lemon, sliced

1 green pepper, chopped

1 tbsp. garlic, minced

2 tbsp. olive oil

1 tbsp. salt

1 tsp. dried thyme

½ tbsp. Dijon mustard

3 lbs. (4 pcs) chicken tenderloins

1 cheddar cheese slice, shredded

4 leaves romaine lettuce

STEPS FOR COOKING

1. Combine the butter, lemon, pepper, garlic, oil, salt, thyme, and mustard in your slow cooker. Switch the slow cooker on high and melt the butter.

2. Add the chicken; ensure to coat the chicken with the butter mixture.

3. Cook on high for 4 hours or on low for 6 hours. Add the cheese and let it sit for 15 minutes on low.

4. To serve, place the chicken over a bed of lettuce leaves.

Salmon with Sauce

Time required:
25 minutes

Servings: 02

INGREDIENTS	STEPS FOR COOKING

INGREDIENTS

1 1/2 lb. Salmon fillet

1 tbsp Duck fat

¾ to 1 tsp. dried dill weed

¾ to 1 tsp. Dried tarragon

Salt and pepper to taste

Cream Sauce:

1/2 tsp. Dried dill weed

1/2 tsp.Dried tarragon

STEPS FOR COOKING

1. Slice the salmon in half and make 2 fillets. Season skin side with salt and pepper and meat of the fish with spices.

2. In a skillet, heat 1 tbsp. duck fat over medium heat.

3. Add salmon to the hot pan, skin side down.

4. Cook the salmon for about 5 minutes. When the skin is crisp, lower the heat and flip salmon.

5. Cook salmon on low heat for 7 to 15 minutes or until your desired doneness is reached.

6. Remove salmon from the pan and set aside.

INGREDIENTS	STEPS FOR COOKING
	7. Add spices and butter to the pan and let brown. Once browned, add cream and mix
	8. Top salmon with sauce and serve.

Bacon-Wrapped Sausages

Time required:
45 minutes

Servings: 04

INGREDIENTS

8 bacon strips

8 sausages

16 pepper jack cheese slices

Salt and ground black pepper, to taste

A pinch of garlic powder

1 teaspoon sweet paprika

1/2 pinch of onion powder

STEPS FOR COOKING

1. Heat up a kitchen grill over medium heat, add the sausages, cook for a few minutes on each side, transfer to a plate, and set aside for a few minutes to cool down.

2. Cut a slit in the middle of each sausage to create pockets, stuff each with 2 cheese slices, and season with salt, pepper, paprika, onion, and garlic powder.

3. Wrap each stuffed sausage in a bacon strip, secure with toothpicks, place on a lined baking sheet, place in an oven at 400ºF, bake for 15 minutes, and serve.

Cauliflower Crust Pizza

Time required:
55 minutes

Servings: 02

INGREDIENTS	STEPS FOR COOKING

For Crust:

1 small head cauliflower, cut into florets

2 large organic eggs, beaten lightly

½ tsp dried oregano

½ tsp garlic powder

Ground black pepper, as required

For Topping:

½ cup sugar-free pizza sauce

¾ cup mozzarella cheese, shredded

¼ cup black olives, pitted and sliced

1. Preheat your oven to 400°F.
2. Line a baking sheet with a lightly greased parchment paper.
3. Add the cauliflower in a food processor and pulse until a rice- like texture is achieved.
4. In a bowl, add the cauliflower rice, eggs, oregano, garlic powder, and black pepper and mix until well combined.
5. Place the cauliflower the mixture in the center of the prepared baking sheet and press with a spatula into a 13-inch thin circle.
6. Then bake for 50 minutes.
7. Remove the baking sheet from the oven. Now, set the oven to broiler on high.

INGREDIENTS	STEPS FOR COOKING

2 tbsp parmesan cheese, grated

8. Place the tomato sauce on top of the pizza crust and spread with a spatula evenly and sprinkle with olives, followed by the cheeses.

9. Broil for about 1 to 2 minutes or until the cheese is bubbly and browned.

10. Remove from oven and, with a pizza cutter, cut the pizza into equal-sized triangles.

11. Serve hot.

Pork Chop with Avocado Salad

Time required:
25 minutes

Servings: 01

INGREDIENTS

For the Chop:

2 teaspoons of coconut oil

1 pork chop (approx. 100 g)

salt

pepper

30 g of cream

½ teaspoon pepper

For the Salad:

¼ head of iceberg lettuce

½ avocado

½ tart apple

½ lemon

1 mild chilli pepper

STEPS FOR COOKING

1. Wash the iceberg lettuce and spin dry. Cut it into thin strips. Remove the core of the avocado. Remove the pulp and chop it into small cubes. Wash the apple. Cut it into four parts, core it and cut it into thin slices.

2. Place the apple in a large bowl with the avocado. Squeeze the lemon and pour it over the avocado and apple strips. Core the chilli pepper.

3. Heat the coconut oil strongly. Wash and dry the chop, then season with salt and pepper on both sides. Then fry it for 3 minutes.

4. For the salad, put the olive oil, mustard, chilli, and coriander in a bowl and stir all the ingredients together. Mix the dressing with

1 teaspoon olive oil
1 teaspoon mustard
½ teaspoon ground coriander salt

iceberg lettuce, avocado and apple and season everything with salt.

5. Take the chop out of the pan. Wrap it in aluminum foil to keep it warm.

6. Loosen the roast with the cream. Add the peppercorns and let the whole boil briefly. Season it with salt and pepper.

7. Serve the chop on a plate and add the sauce and salad.

Vegetarian Borscht

Time required:
35 minutes

Servings: 04

INGREDIENTS

1 leek

500 g beetroot

3 carrots

500 g white cabbage

500 g potatoes

1 onion

2 tbsp sunflower oil

2 tbsp balsamic
vinegar (white)

½ bunch of dill

1 cup of sour cream

1 ½ l of broth

Salt, pepper, sugar

STEPS FOR COOKING

1. Clean and chop the vegetables. Cut
   the beetroot (with gloves!) In pencils,
   leek in rings, carrots in slices, white
   cabbage in strips, dice the potatoes
   and chop the onion.

2. Briefly sauté everything except the
   carrots and the leek in oil. Cover and
   simmer for about 15 minutes and
   then add the carrots and leek. Let
   simmer for another 10 minutes.
   Season to taste with sugar, vinegar,
   salt and pepper.

3. Serve with sour cream and some dill.

Greek Redfish Fillet

Time required:
35 minutes

Servings: 02

INGREDIENTS	STEPS FOR COOKING

2 redfish fillets

10 olives

Main courses

1 tablespoon lemon juice

50g chopped tomatoes

1 onion oregano

1 clove of garlic basil

1 teaspoon olive oil

Salt and pepper

1. Preheat the oven to 180 ° C, prepare a baking dish and use the fish and the pour in lemon juice.

2. Peel the onion and garlic, chop them into small pieces and then fry them in a pan with olive oil.

3. Add the chopped tomatoes, mix well, add salt, pepper and season the herbs and stir well.

4. Pour the mixture over the fish fillet and put everything in the oven for about 30 minutes.

Asian Noodle Soup with Prawns and Chantenay Carrots

Time required:
25 minutes

Servings: 04

INGREDIENTS	STEPS FOR COOKING

INGREDIENTS

1tbsp rapeseed oil

2 garlic cloves, peeled and sliced

2 tsp ginger, peeled and grated

1 tsp chili flakes

1 green chilli, sliced

1 peeled and finely chopped stalk of lemongrass

150g of sliced Chantenay carrots

6 sliced shitake mushrooms

2 tbsp of fish sauce

1 liter chicken stock

STEPS FOR COOKING

1. In a medium-sized pan, heat the oil. Cook for 1 minute, stirring continuously, until the chili flakes, garlic, ginger, green chili, and lemongrass have softened.

2. Cook for another minute after adding the sliced Chantenay carrots and shitake mushrooms, as well as a splash of fish sauce.

3. Bring the stock to a boil, then insert the noodles, prawns, spring onion and proceed to cook for another 4 minutes.

4. Stir in the soy sauce, coriander, hot chili sauce, lime juice, and sesame oil after removing the pan from the oven.

INGREDIENTS	STEPS FOR COOKING
150g of pre-soaked rice noodles *24 peeled and de-veined prawns* *4 sliced spring onions* *½ bunch of chopped coriander* *1 tbsp of dark soy sauce* *1 tbsp of sweet chili sauce Juice of 2 limes* *1 tsp of sesame oil*	5. Taste and season to taste; you may want to add a pinch of sweet chili and/or fish sauce.

Pork Carnitas

Time required:
1 hour 20
minutes

Servings: 04

INGREDIENTS

2 ½ pounds of boneless pork shoulder, cut into 4 large pieces

6 medium garlic cloves, minced

2 teaspoons of ground cumin

1 teaspoon of smoked paprika

3 chipotle peppers in adobo sauce, minced

1 teaspoon of dried oregano

2 bay leaves

STEPS FOR COOKING

1. Season the pork shoulder with sea salt, black pepper, ground cumin, dried oregano, and smoked paprika.

2. Press the "Sauté" setting on your Instant Pot and add the olive oil.

3. Once hot, add the pork pieces and sear for 4 minutes per side or until brown.

4. Add the remaining ingredients inside your Instant Pot. Lock the lid and cook at high pressure for 80 minutes. When the cooking is done, quick release the pressure and remove the lid.

5. Carefully shred the pork using two forks and continue to stir until well coated with the liquid.

INGREDIENTS	STEPS FOR COOKING
1 cup of homemade low-sodium chicken broth *Fine sea salt and freshly cracked black pepper (to taste)* *2 tablespoons of olive oil*	6. Remove the bay leave and adjust the seasoning if necessary. Serve and enjoy!

Single Skillet Seafood-Filled Frittata

Time required:
25 minutes

Servings: 04

INGREDIENTS

1 green pepper

¼ lime, squeezed for juice

1 tbsp. coconut flour

1 tbsp. sesame oil

1 tbsp. soy sauce, gluten-free

1 tbsp. coconut oil

3 bulbs fresh onions, chopped

½ clove garlic, minced

¼ cup prawns, raw

11/3 cup mussels, deshelled

2 eggs whisked

STEPS FOR COOKING

1. Preheat your oven to 475 °F. Meanwhile, make the sauce by combining the first five ingredients in a mixing bowl. Mix thoroughly until fully combined. Set aside.

2. Melt the coconut oil in a small skillet and fry the onions. Add the garlic, prawns, and mussels. Cook for 10 minutes until the prawns turn pink.

3. Stir in the eggs. Place the skillet in the oven and bake for 5 minutes.

4. Slice the frittata into four slices and serve with the sauce.

Octopus Salad

Time required:
55 minutes

Servings: 02

INGREDIENTS	STEPS FOR COOKING

21 ounces octopus, rinsed Juice of 1 lemon

4 celery stalks, chopped

3 ounces olive oil

Salt and ground black pepper, to taste

4 tablespoons fresh parsley, chopped

1. Put the octopus in a pot, add enough water to cover them, cover the pot, bring to a boil over medium heat, cook for 40 minutes, drain, and set aside to cool down.

2. Chop the octopus and put it in a salad bowl.

3. Add the celery stalks, parsley, oil, and lemon juice, and toss well.

4. Season with salt and pepper, toss again, and serve.

Couscous with Figs and Vegetable Ragout

Time required:
25 minutes

Servings: 01

INGREDIENTS

2 dried figs

1 small red onion

½ zucchini

½ stick of leek

2 tbsp olive oil

1 tbsp tomato paste

70 ml vegetable stock

1 tbsp lemon juice

1 teaspoon ground cumin

70 g couscous

1 sprig of fresh mint

salt

pepper

STEPS FOR COOKING

1. Cut the figs into small cubes. Peel the onion and finely chop it. Wash, clean, and cut the zucchini and leek into thin strips. Heat 1 tablespoon of olive oil in a saucepan and simmer everything together over low heat for 2 minutes. Add tomato paste and pour stock over it. Add the lemon juice and cumin and season with salt and pepper. Cook the vegetables over low heat for 15 minutes.

2. Boil water in a saucepan and add salt and olive oil. As soon as the water boils, take the pan off the stove and add the couscous. Wash the mint. Dry them and roughly chop them.

INGREDIENTS	STEPS FOR COOKING
	3. Serve the couscous with the vegetables and sprinkle with the mint.

Chicken Soup

Time required:
55 minutes

Servings: 02

INGREDIENTS	STEPS FOR COOKING

INGREDIENTS

750 g carrots
150 g potatoes
2 onions
2 tablespoons oil
1 tbsp vegetable stock Paprika powder
150 g chicken fillets

STEPS FOR COOKING

1. First, peel the carrots and potatoes and cut them into small pieces. Now peel the onion and cut into cubes.

2. Then heat the oil in a saucepan and sauté the onions, potatoes and carrots. Pour approx. 1 liter of hot water into the pot and add the vegetable stock.

3. Now season everything well and then let the soup boil for 25 minutes. Carefully wash the chicken fillets, cut them into small pieces and fry them in a pan with hot oil.

4. Puree the contents of the pot after the cooking time and arrange on a plate. Then add the fried chicken fillets.

Green Pasta with Chicken

Time required:
35 minutes

Servings: 02

INGREDIENTS	STEPS FOR COOKING

600g chicken fillet
1 teaspoon vegetable stock
Chicken breast fillet
3tsp tomato paste
2 zucchini
200g goat cheese
5 tomatoes
Salt and pepper
2 tablespoons of olive oil

1. Wash the chicken fillet, cut into small pieces, into one Pan give and with olive oil and a tablespoon of water fry.
2. Wash zucchini and peel and with a potato peeler in small spaghetti.
3. Take the chicken out of the pan, leave the juice in the pan, the spaghetti
4. in the pan give and with a little vegetable stock and brown water.
5. Cut the tomatoes into small cubes and add the tomato paste to the pan
6. give the goat cheese and the chicken fillets in the pan give and spice up with salt and pepper

Shallot and Potato Cake

Time required:
95 minutes

Servings: 06

INGREDIENTS

4 large potatoes

4 large Echalion shallots

1 tbsp olive oil and

1 tbsp butter

1 tsp butter for greasing

1 egg, beaten

2 tbsp sour cream

Nutmeg

Thyme

STEPS FOR COOKING

1. Preheat the oven to 200°F. Then bake the potatoes along with their skins for an hour or more, until thoroughly baked. Allow time for cooling.

2. Peel and cut the shallots, then sauté for up to 40 minutes in the oil and butter until smooth and golden.

3. In the meantime, cut the cold potatoes in half and scoop out the flesh into some kind of bowl, breaking it up with a fork. Season with salt and pepper and stir in the beaten egg, sour cream, and a grating of nutmeg. Mix in the fried shallots softly.

4. Butter a cake pan and pour the batter into it.

5. Preheat oven to 350°F and bake for 30 minutes, or until golden brown.

INGREDIENTS	STEPS FOR COOKING
	6. Remove from the oven and set aside to cool slightly before turning out with a knife around the edge. Insert a few thyme leaves to finish.

Teriyaki Salmon

Time required:
25 minutes

Servings: 02

INGREDIENTS	STEPS FOR COOKING
3 tbsps. lime juice *2 tbsps. olive oil* *2 tbsps. reduced-sodium teriyaki sauce* *1 tbsp. balsamic vinegar* *1 tbsp. Dijon mustard* *1 tsp. garlic powder* *6 drops hot pepper sauce* *6 uncooked jumbo salmon*	1. Mix the first 7 ingredients together in a big zip lock plastic bag then put in the shrimp. Seal the zip lock bag and turn to coat the salmon. Keep in the fridge for an hour and occasionally turn. 2. Drain the marinated salmon and discard marinade. Broil the salmon 4 inches from heat for 3 to 4 minutes per side or until the salmon turn pink in color.

Asparagus and Cheese on Toast Eggy Bread Combo

Time required:
15 minutes

Servings: 02

INGREDIENTS	STEPS FOR COOKING
250g asparagus tips *4 slices crusty bread* *150g grated cheese; cheddar, gruyere, red Leicester or a combination* *2 beaten eggs* *Sea salt & black pepper* *1 tbsp chopped chives*	1. Heat the oven to 180 2. Trim the asparagus tips as well as blanch them in boiling water for a few seconds before rinsing them in cool water. 3. Toast the bread lightly in the toaster and set it aside to cool. Mix the beaten eggs with the grated cheese. 4. Spread the cheese & egg mixture evenly around the four slices of bread, going all the way to the ends. 5. Bake the bread for five minutes on a baking sheet. Remove the asparagus spears from the baking sheet and place them in the hot cheese mixture. Return the tray to the oven for five

INGREDIENTS	STEPS FOR COOKING
	minutes more, or when the cheese has puffed up and is bubbling.
	6. Serve with a sprinkling of chopped chives.

Garlic Butter Beef Steak

Time required:
25 minutes

Servings: 02

INGREDIENTS

1 pound of beef sirloin steaks

½ cup of red wine

4 tablespoons of unsalted butter

2 tablespoons of fresh parsley, finely chopped

4 medium garlic cloves, peeled and minced

Fine sea salt and freshly cracked black pepper (to taste)

STEPS FOR COOKING

1. Season the beef steaks with sea salt and freshly cracked black pepper.

2. Press the "Sauté" setting on your Instant Pot and add the butter. Once melted, add the beef steaks and sear for 2 minutes per side or until brown.

3. Pour in the red wine and fresh parsley. Lock the lid and cook at high pressure for 12 minutes. When the cooking is done, naturally release the pressure and carefully remove the lid.

4. Top the steak with the butter sauce. Serve and enjoy!

Stuffed Straw Mushroom Mobcap

Time required:
25 minutes

Servings: 01

1 cup fresh spinach washed, bathed in ice, and drained

1 cup straw mushrooms or Chinese mushroom washed and stems removed

1 tbsp. coconut oil

1 bulb onion, finely chopped

1 clove garlic, minced

A dash of salt and pepper

A pinch of nutmeg

¼ cup quinoa, cooked

1. Spread the spinach leaves over the food film while rolling them.
2. Fry the mushrooms with coconut oil in a saucepan before adding onion and garlic. Season with pepper, salt, and nutmeg. Set aside.
3. Combine the cooked quinoa with cottage cheese. Spread the mixture evenly on the spinach leaves then roll into a pudding with the help of the food film.
4. Stuff the mushroom heads with the spinach pudding, and place them in the fridge.
5. Just before serving, slice the mushroom head with a sharp knife and pass quickly to the pan to heat.

INGREDIENTS	STEPS FOR COOKING
3.5 oz. cottage cheese	

Lumb Curry

Time required:
25 minutes

___

Servings: 01

INGREDIENTS

2 tbsp. grated Fresh ginger

2 cloves Garlic peeled and minced

2 tsp. Cardamom

1 Onion –peeled and chopped

6 Cloves

1-pound Lamb meat cubed

2 tsp. Cumin powder

1 tsp. Garam Masala

½ tsp. Chili powder

1 tsp. Turmeric

2 tsp. Coriander

1 pound Spinach Canned

STEPS FOR COOKING

1. In a slow cooker, mix lamb with tomatoes, spinach, ginger, garlic, onion, cardamom, cloves, cumin, garam masala, chili, turmeric, and coriander.

2. Uncover the slow cooker, stir the chili, divide into bowls, and serve.

Cabbage Casserole

Time required:
55 minutes

Servings: 02

INGREDIENTS

½ head cabbage

2 scallions, chopped

4 tbsp unsalted butter

2 ounces cream cheese, softened

¼ cup parmesan cheese, grated

¼ cup fresh cream

½ tsp Dijon mustard

2 tbsp fresh parsley, chopped

Salt and ground black pepper, as required

STEPS FOR COOKING

1. Preheat your oven to 350°F.

2. Cut the cabbage head in half, lengthwise. Then cut into 4 equal-sized wedges.

3. In a pan of boiling water, add cabbage wedges and cook, cover for about 5 minutes.

4. Drain well and arrange cabbage wedges into a small baking dish.

5. In a small pan, melt butter and sauté onions for about 5 minutes.

6. Add the remaining ingredients and stir to combine.

7. Remove from the heat and immediately place the cheese mixture over cabbage wedges evenly.

8. Bake for about 20 minutes.

9. Remove from the oven and let it cool for about 5 minutes before serving.
10. Cut into 3 equal-sized portions and serve.

Lobster Bisque

Time required:
1 hour

Servings: 04

INGREDIENTS

4 garlic cloves, peeled and minced

1 onion, peeled and chopped

24 ounces lobster chunks, precooked

Salt and ground black pepper, to taste

½ cup tomato paste

2 carrots, diced

4 celery stalks, chopped

1-quart seafood stock

1 tablespoon olive oil

1 cup heavy cream

STEPS FOR COOKING

1. Heat up a pot with the oil over medium heat, add the onion, stir, and cook for 4 minutes.

2. Add the garlic, stir, and cook for 1 minute. Add the celery and carrot, stir, and cook for 1 minute.

3. Add the tomato paste, and stock, and stir.

4. Add the bay leaves, salt, pepper, peppercorns, paprika, thyme, and xanthan gum, stir, and simmer over medium heat for 1 hour.

5. Discard bay leaves, add the cream, and bring to a simmer.

6. Blend using an immersion blender, add the lobster chunks, and cook for a few minutes.

INGREDIENTS	STEPS FOR COOKING
3 bay leaves *1 teaspoon dried thyme* *1 teaspoon peppercorns* *1 teaspoon paprika* *1 teaspoon xanthan gum* *½ cup fresh parsley, chopped* *1 tablespoon lemon juice*	7. Add the lemon juice, stir, divide into bowls, and sprinkle parsley on top.

Creamy Pea Soup with Coriander

Time required:
45 minutes

Servings: 02

INGREDIENTS

450 g frozen peas

1 onion

2 tbsp olive oil

600 ml vegetable stock

200 ml whipped cream

1 bunch of coriander

STEPS FOR COOKING

1. Heat olive oil in a pan and fry the onion in it until translucent. Add 300 g of peas and deglaze them with vegetable stock. Season the soup with salt and pepper and let it simmer covered for 8 minutes.

2. Wash the coriander sprigs and pat them dry. Roughly chop them and add them to the pan with the whipped cream. Puree the soup with a hand blender and strain it through a sieve.

3. Just before serving, add 150 g peas and heat the soup again for 3 minutes. Garnish with coriander and serve warm.

Zuppa Toscana with Cauliflower

Time required:
35 minutes

Servings: 04

1-pound ground Italian sausage

6 cups homemade low-sodium chicken stock

2 cups cauliflower florets

1 onion, finely chopped

1 cup kale, stemmed and roughly chopped

1 (14.5-ounce) can of full-fat coconut milk

¼ teaspoon of sea salt

¼ teaspoon freshly cracked black pepper

1. On the Instant Pot, press "Sauté" and add the ground Italian sausage. Cook until brown, stirring occasionally and breaking up the meat with a wooden spoon.

2. Add the remaining ingredients except for the kale and coconut milk and stir until well combined.

3. Cover and cook for 10 minutes on high pressure. When done, release the pressure naturally and remove the lid. Stir in the kale and coconut milk. Cover and sit for 5 minutes or until the kale has wilted. Serve and enjoy!

Naked Whisky Mac Gateau

Time required:
45 minutes

Servings: 02

INGREDIENTS

300 g plain flour

10 g bicarbonate soda

4 tsp of ground ginger

2 tsp of ground spice mixed

300 g soft slightly brown sugar

Three medium-sized beaten eggs,

300 ml buttermilk

175 g very soft unsalted butter,

3 tiny oranges

300 ml double cream

5 tbsp whisky

2 tbsp clear honey

STEPS FOR COOKING

1. Heat oven at 180°C.

2. Start by greasing and lining the three x 18 cm tins of sandwich cake. In a mixing bowl, sift together the bicarbonate of the soda., Flour and spices, and whisk in brown sugar.

3. Mix in the buttermilk, potatoes, and butter until the batter is smooth and dense. Divide the batter between the muffin tins, smooth surfaces, & bake for thirty -35 minutes, or till golden & firm.

4. Rind from 1 of oranges is to be grated and then set aside for decoration. Remove the tops & bottoms of all oranges, then peel away rind & pith while leaving the oranges intact. Then thinly slice them.

5. Whip cream till it begins to peak, and add orange rind, two tablespoons,

INGREDIENTS	STEPS FOR COOKING
orange wedges and Ice-covered rosemary sprigs to decorate	whisky & honey. Using a cocktail tip, prick cakes and drizzle with the leftover whisky. Then sprinkle whipped cream on two of the cakes. Drain and layer orange slices on top of the milk.

6. Place the cakes on a plate and stack them on top of one another. Use a palette knife to finely scatter some of the remaining cream across the edge of cake, leaving cake layers visible. Spread the remaining cream on the top. Then garnish with the orange wedges & frosted rosemary before serving.

Pulled Pork Breakfast Hash

Time required:
15 minutes

Servings: 02

INGREDIENTS	STEPS FOR COOKING

2 tablespoons of olive oil

1 turnip, finely chopped

2 tablespoons of red onion, finely chopped

½ cup of cooked pulled pork

2 large organic eggs

1 cup of kale, stemmed and roughly chopped

4 brussel sprouts, halved

1 teaspoon of smoked paprika

1. Press the "Sauté" function on your Instant Pot and add the olive oil, turnips and onions. Cook until the vegetables have softened, stirring occasionally.

2. Add the seasoning and remaining vegetables.

3. Add the pulled pork and cook for another 2 minutes.

4. Remove all the contents and transfer to an oven-proof dish that fits inside your Instant Pot.

5. Create two separate divots into the dish and crack the eggs. Cover with aluminum foil.

6. Add 2 cups of water and a trivet to your Instant Pot. Lock the lid and cook at high pressure for 3 minutes.

INGREDIENTS	STEPS FOR COOKING

1 teaspoon of fine sea salt

1 teaspoon of freshly cracked black pepper

7. Check if the eggs are set. Serve and enjoy!

Chocolate Walnut Cookies

Time required:
35 minutes

Servings: 06

INGREDIENTS

1/4 cup coconut oil
3 tbsp. sweetener
4 tbsp. unsalted butter
1 cup sugar-free chocolate chips
1 cup coconut flakes
1/2 cup pecans
1/2 cup walnuts
1 tsp. vanilla extract
4 egg yolks
Sea salt

STEPS FOR COOKING

1. Take a bowl and mix coconut oil, butter, sweetener, chocolate chips, vanilla extract, egg yolks, coconut, and walnuts. Stir well.

2. Use a scope to make a cookie and drop an even amount of dough on the baking pan.

3. Sprinkle salt as per taste and bake for 12 minutes in a preheated oven at 350 °F until golden brown.

Cottage Pie

Time required:
25 minutes

Servings: 10

INGREDIENTS

3 tablespoons olive oil

2 cloves garlic crushed

1 tablespoon dried oregano

1 teaspoon salt

2 pounds ground beef

3 tablespoons tomato paste

1 cup beef stock

1/4 cup red wine vinegar

2 tablespoons fresh thyme leaves

STEPS FOR COOKING

1. Place a large saucepan over a high heat. Add the olive oil, garlic, oregano, onion and celery and Sauté for 5 minutes, until the onion is starting to become translucent.

2. Add the salt and ground beef, stirring continuously to break apart the meat while it browns. When the beef is browned add the tomato paste and stir well. Add the beef stock and red wine vinegar and simmer uncovered for 20 minutes until the liquid has reduced.

3. Add the thyme and green beans and simmer for 5 minutes before removing from the heat. Spoon the beef mixture into your casserole dish and set aside.

INGREDIENTS	STEPS FOR COOKING

10 ounces green beans, cut into 1in lengths

Topping:

1.5 pounds cauliflower cut into florets

3 ounces butter

1/2 teaspoon salt

1/4 teaspoon pepper

3 egg yolks

Pinch paprika

Pinch dried oregano

4. Preheat your oven to 175C/350F. Topping: Fill a large saucepan two-thirds full of water and bring to the boil. Add the cauliflower and cook for 7-10 minutes until tender. Carefully pour the water and cauliflower into a colander and drain well. Return the drained cauliflower to the saucepan, along with the butter, salt and pepper. Using your stick blender, blend the cauliflower into a smooth mash. Add the egg yolks and blend well.

5. Gently spoon the mashed cauliflower onto the beef mixture in your casserole dish. Sprinkle with paprika and oregano.

6. Bake the pie in the oven for 25-30 minutes, until the mash is golden brown. Serve immediately or chill and store in the fridge for up to 1 week.

Chia Seed Banana Blueberry Delight

Time required:
30 minutes

Servings: 02

INGREDIENTS

1 cup yogurt
½ cup blueberries
½ tsp salt
½ tsp cinnamon
1 banana
1 tsp vanilla extract
1/4 cup chia seeds

STEPS FOR COOKING

1. Discard the skin of the banana and cut into semi-thick circles, or mash if you would like.

2. Clean the blueberries properly and rinse well.

3. Soak the chia seeds in water for 30 minutes or longer then drain and transfer into a bowl.

4. Add the yogurt and mix well.

5. Add the salt, cinnamon, and vanilla then mix again.

6. Now fold in the bananas and blueberries gently.

7. If you want, add dried fruit or nuts, then serve immediately.

Simple Vanilla Hemp

Time required:
15 minutes

Servings: 02

INGREDIENTS	STEPS FOR COOKING

INGREDIENTS

1 cup water

1 cup unsweetened
hemp milk, vanilla

1 and ½ tablespoons
coconut oil,
unrefined

½ cup frozen
blueberries, mixed

4 cup leafy greens,
kale and spinach

1 tablespoon
flaxseeds

1 tablespoon
almond butter

STEPS FOR COOKING

1. Add listed ingredients to blender
2. Blend until you have a smooth and creamy texture
3. Serve chilled and enjoy!

Wiener Rahmschmarrn

Time required:
55 minutes

Servings: 02

INGREDIENTS

1 tbsp raisins

20 ml rum

¼ cup of sour cream

1 large egg

2 tbsp sugar

30 grams of flour

½ teaspoon baking powder

1 pinch of salt

1 tbsp butter

1 tbsp almond flakes

some powdered sugar

STEPS FOR COOKING

1. Soak the raisins in rum and let them steep for 30 minutes.

2. Preheat the oven to 180 ° C. Separate the egg. Put the egg yolks in a bowl with 1 tablespoon of sugar, flour and baking powder and stir everything into a smooth batter. Beat the egg whites until stiff. Fold them into the batter.

3. Melt the butter in a pan and sprinkle the flaked almonds on top. Put in the batter. Scatter the raisins and the remaining sugar on top.

4. Take the pan out of the oven and let the batter cool down a bit. Cut it into large pieces and sprinkle with powdered sugar.

Chocolate Coconut Pudding

Time required:
25 minutes

Servings: 02

INGREDIENTS

400ml almond milk

1 tablespoon of cocoa

2 tablespoons cornstarch

3 tablespoons coconut flakes

1 pinch of stevia

STEPS FOR COOKING

1. 6 tbsp of the almond milk with cocoa powder, coconut flakes, corn starch and stevia with a whisk mix and the remaining almond milk in a pot to cook bring.

2. Once the almond milk boiled is the cocoa-starch mixture to the milk type and with a whisk 30 seconds under constant stir to simmer.

3. From the hot stove take and in bowls distribute.

Quesadilla Pancakes

Time required:
45 minutes

Servings: 04

INGREDIENTS

red peppers, chopped into small pieces

140g red Leicester, grated

4 tbsp chopped fresh coriander

8 pre-made pancakes

1 tbsp butter

1 garlic clove, crushed

½ tsp ground cumin

400g can of kidney beans, drained juice one lemon

1 red chilli, deseeded if you don't like it

STEPS FOR COOKING

1. Preheat oven to 180C.

2. Then spread the cheese, peppers, and coriander over four pancakes. All should be seasoned properly so that each one is covered with another pancake to prepare a sandwich.

3. Put the quesadilla pancakes on the baking sheets and cook them for more than five minutes in the oven until the cheese starts to melt.

4. The butter is to be warmed in a saucepan. Next, insert the garlic and cook for one minute till fragrant.

5. Next, add the cumin and beans. Mix for two minutes. Then mash roughly. Stir through half the lemon juice. Then spoon into a serving dish and top with the chili.

INGREDIENTS	STEPS FOR COOKING
too hot, sliced (optional) *2 avocados, sliced* *2 Little Gem lettuces, sliced*	6. Finally, put the avocado in the remaining lemon juice. 7. Finally, when ready, serve the quesadillas with lettuce, beans, and avocado.

Low-Carb Pancake Crepes

Time required:
20 minutes

Servings: 02

INGREDIENTS

3ounces cream cheese

1 tsp ground cinnamon

1 tbsp honey

1 tsp ground cardamom

1 tsp butter

2 egg, beaten

STEPS FOR COOKING

1. In a bowl, whisk the eggs finely.
2. Beat the cream cheese in a different bowl until it becomes soft.
3. Add the egg mixture to the softened cream cheese and mix well until there are no lumps left.
4. Add cinnamon, cardamom, and honey to it. Mix well. The batter would be runnier than that of pancake batter.
5. In a pan, add the butter and set over medium heat.
6. Add the batter using a scooper, that way size of the crepes will be the same and fry.
7. Repeat the process.
8. Drizzle some honey on top and enjoy.

Almond Shortbread Cookies

Time required:
25 minutes

Servings: 06

INGREDIENTS

1/3 cup coconut flour

1/4 cup erythritol

2/3 cup almond flour

8 drops stevia

1/2 cup butter

1 tsp. almond or vanilla extract

1/4 tsp. baking powder

For Glaze:

1/4 cup coconut butter

8 drops stevia

STEPS FOR COOKING

1. In a bowl, add coconut flour, almond flour, erythritol, baking powder. Add vanilla or almond extract, stevia, and melted butter.

2. Make a soft dough. The dough must be divided into two and chill in the refrigerator for 10 minutes.

3. Roll the dough on a sheet and cut cookies with the help of a cookie cutter.

4. Place cookies into a baking pan and bake for 6 minutes in a preheated oven at 180C.

5. Let the cookies completely cool and apply the glaze.

Banana and Raspberry Ice Cream

Time required:
25 minutes

Servings: 02

INGREDIENTS	STEPS FOR COOKING

2 bananas

5 tablespoons of yogurt 100g raspberries

1. Peel banana and cut in thin slices, wash the raspberry and depositions over night or at least for 4 hours in the freezer to give.
2. Take the frozen fruit out of the freezer and put together with the Put the yogurt in a blender.
3. All ingredients puree until a uniform mass emerged is.

9 781802 611106